MW01101876

A MOVIE
LOVER'S
DIARY

MOVIE LOVER ___M . phil_____

DIARY KEPT BETWEEN ___Aug 2012___ AND _____

A MOVIE
LOVER'S
DIARY

FIREFLY BOOKS

A Movie Lover's Diary
ISBN 1-55209-148-1

🏚
A Firefly Book

Published by Firefly Books Ltd., 3680 Victoria Park Avenue,
Willowdale, Ontario, Canada M2H 3K1

Published in the U.S. by Firefly Books (U.S.) Inc.
P.O. Box 1338, Ellicott Station, Buffalo, New York 14205

Conceived and edited by Shelagh Wallace
Design and original illustrations by Scott McKowen

Acknowledgements
We wish to thank those publishers who have given their permission
to reproduce excerpts from works still in copyright. If anyone has been
unintentionally omitted, we offer our apologies and ask that you notify
the publisher so you may be included in future editions.

Quotations from *Colombo's Hollywood: Wit and Wisdom of the Moviemakers*
by John Robert Colombo. Reprinted by kind permission of the author.

Quotations from *Halliwell's Filmgoer's Companion*, Eighth Edition, edited
by John Walker and published by HarperCollins Publishers in 1985.

Quotation by Henry Jaglom reprinted by permission of St. Martin's Press
Incorporated from *Movies for a Desert Isle* by Ellen Oumano copyright
©1987.

Quotation by Garth Drabinsky reprinted by permission of Garth H.
Drabinsky, O.C., Chairman and C.E.O., Livent Inc.

Quotation by Woody Allen reprinted by permission of Simon & Schuster
from *Seventeen Interviews Film Stars and Superstars* by Ed Miller. Copyright
©1970 by Triangle Publications Inc.

Printed in Canada

TABLE OF CONTENTS

Young man, you should be grateful, since, although my invention is not for sale, it would undoubtedly ruin you. It can be exploited for a certain time as a scientific curiosity, but, apart from that, it has no commercial value whatsoever. AUGUSTE LUMIÈRE, 1895

I consider that the greatest mission of the motion picture is first to make people happy... to bring more joy and cheer and wholesome good will into this world of ours. And God knows we need it. THOMAS A. EDISON

I REALLY
WANT
TO SEE...

E dison is the new Gutenberg. He has invented the new printing. The state that realizes this may lead the soul of America, day after tomorrow. VACHEL LINDSAY

The cinema is for us the most important instrument of all the arts. NIKOLAI LENIN

---

believe that motion pictures are the most vital influence upon public thought in the world today. ADELE ROGERS ST. JOHNS

17

*O*n the spiritual plane, the cinema is an
invention every whit as important as,
on the material plane, the freeing of
nuclear energy. JEAN DEBRIX

MOVIES TO SEE BY CAST / CREW

They have slipped into the American mind more misinformation in one evening than the Dark Ages could muster in a decade.

BEN HECHT

M
ovies are fun, but they're not a cure for cancer. WARREN BEATTY

I only went to college because my parents couldn't imagine it otherwise. I enrolled in NYU as a motion picture major. I didn't know anything about it at all and had no interest in it except that I had been movie-crazy as a kid. I went to the movies every day – a double bill, seven days a week.

WOODY ALLEN

SEEN ANY
GOOD MOVIES
LATELY?

TITLE

CAST / CREW

STUDIO / YEAR

THEATER / VIDEO / TV   Netflix!

REVIEW

RECOMMENDED BY / TO

TITLE

CAST / CREW

STUDIO / YEAR

THEATER / VIDEO / TV

REVIEW

RECOMMENDED BY / TO

TITLE

CAST / CREW

STUDIO / YEAR

THEATER / VIDEO / TV

REVIEW

RECOMMENDED BY / TO

TITLE

CAST / CREW

STUDIO / YEAR

THEATER / VIDEO / TV

REVIEW

RECOMMENDED BY / TO

TITLE

CAST / CREW

STUDIO / YEAR

THEATER / VIDEO / TV

REVIEW

RECOMMENDED BY / TO

A movie is like a person. Either you trust it or you don't. MIKE NICHOLS

TITLE

CAST / CREW

STUDIO / YEAR

THEATER / VIDEO / TV

REVIEW

RECOMMENDED BY / TO

TITLE

CAST / CREW

STUDIO / YEAR

THEATER / VIDEO / TV

REVIEW

RECOMMENDED BY / TO

TITLE

CAST / CREW

STUDIO / YEAR

THEATER / VIDEO / TV

REVIEW

RECOMMENDED BY / TO

TITLE

CAST / CREW

STUDIO / YEAR

THEATER / VIDEO / TV

REVIEW

RECOMMENDED BY / TO

TITLE

CAST / CREW

STUDIO / YEAR

THEATER / VIDEO / TV

REVIEW

RECOMMENDED BY / TO

TITLE

CAST / CREW

STUDIO / YEAR

THEATER / VIDEO / TV

REVIEW

RECOMMENDED BY / TO

TITLE

CAST / CREW

STUDIO / YEAR

THEATER / VIDEO / TV

REVIEW

RECOMMENDED BY / TO

TITLE

CAST / CREW

STUDIO / YEAR

THEATER / VIDEO / TV

REVIEW

RECOMMENDED BY / TO

The successful picture, big or small, has to make you do one of three things. Sit on the edge of your seat, laugh a lot or reach for your handkerchief. I used to have a gag man who claimed there were only two kinds of films. Slouch and sit up. DARRYL F. ZANUCK

TITLE

CAST / CREW

STUDIO / YEAR

THEATER / VIDEO / TV

REVIEW

RECOMMENDED BY / TO

TITLE

CAST / CREW

STUDIO / YEAR

THEATER / VIDEO / TV

REVIEW

RECOMMENDED BY / TO

TITLE

CAST / CREW

STUDIO / YEAR

THEATER / VIDEO / TV

REVIEW

RECOMMENDED BY / TO

TITLE

CAST / CREW

STUDIO / YEAR

THEATER / VIDEO / TV

REVIEW

RECOMMENDED BY / TO

TITLE

CAST / CREW

STUDIO / YEAR

THEATER / VIDEO / TV

REVIEW

RECOMMENDED BY / TO

TITLE

CAST / CREW

STUDIO / YEAR

THEATER / VIDEO / TV

REVIEW

RECOMMENDED BY / TO

TITLE

CAST / CREW

STUDIO / YEAR

THEATER / VIDEO / TV

REVIEW

RECOMMENDED BY / TO

TITLE

CAST / CREW

STUDIO / YEAR

THEATER / VIDEO / TV

REVIEW

RECOMMENDED BY / TO

TITLE

CAST / CREW

STUDIO / YEAR

THEATER / VIDEO / TV

REVIEW

RECOMMENDED BY / TO

TITLE

CAST / CREW

STUDIO / YEAR

THEATER / VIDEO / TV

REVIEW

RECOMMENDED BY / TO

TITLE

CAST / CREW

STUDIO / YEAR

THEATER / VIDEO / TV

REVIEW

RECOMMENDED BY / TO

A good film is when the price of dinner, the theater admission, and the babysitter were worth it. ALFRED HITCHCOCK

TITLE

CAST / CREW

STUDIO / YEAR

THEATER / VIDEO / TV

REVIEW

RECOMMENDED BY / TO

TITLE

CAST / CREW

STUDIO / YEAR

THEATER / VIDEO / TV

REVIEW

RECOMMENDED BY / TO

TITLE

CAST / CREW

STUDIO / YEAR

THEATER / VIDEO / TV

REVIEW

RECOMMENDED BY / TO

TITLE

CAST / CREW

STUDIO / YEAR

THEATER / VIDEO / TV

REVIEW

RECOMMENDED BY / TO

TITLE

CAST / CREW

STUDIO / YEAR

THEATER / VIDEO / TV

REVIEW

RECOMMENDED BY / TO

TITLE

CAST / CREW

STUDIO / YEAR

THEATER / VIDEO / TV

REVIEW

RECOMMENDED BY / TO

TITLE

CAST / CREW

STUDIO / YEAR

THEATER / VIDEO / TV

REVIEW

RECOMMENDED BY / TO

TITLE

CAST / CREW

STUDIO / YEAR

THEATER / VIDEO / TV

REVIEW

RECOMMENDED BY / TO

TITLE

CAST / CREW

STUDIO / YEAR

THEATER / VIDEO / TV

REVIEW

RECOMMENDED BY / TO

TITLE

CAST / CREW

STUDIO / YEAR

THEATER / VIDEO / TV

REVIEW

RECOMMENDED BY / TO

TITLE

CAST / CREW

STUDIO / YEAR

THEATER / VIDEO / TV   .

REVIEW

RECOMMENDED BY / TO

TITLE

CAST / CREW

STUDIO / YEAR

THEATER / VIDEO / TV

REVIEW

RECOMMENDED BY / TO

TITLE

CAST / CREW

STUDIO / YEAR

THEATER / VIDEO / TV

REVIEW

RECOMMENDED BY / TO

TITLE

CAST / CREW

STUDIO / YEAR

THEATER / VIDEO / TV

REVIEW

RECOMMENDED BY / TO

TITLE

CAST / CREW

STUDIO / YEAR

THEATER / VIDEO / TV

REVIEW

RECOMMENDED BY / TO

CAST / CREW:

TITLE   DATE SEEN

F
or an actress to be a success, she must have
the face of Venus, the brains of Minerva, the
grace of Terpsichore, the memory of Macaulay,
the figure of Juno, and the hide of a rhinoceros.

ETHEL BARRYMORE

CAST / CREW:

TITLE	DATE SEEN

CAST / CREW:

TITLE	DATE SEEN

CAST / CREW:

TITLE	DATE SEEN

CAST / CREW:

TITLE	DATE SEEN

*an't act. Can't sing. Slightly bald.
Can dance a little.* FRED ASTAIRE'S SCREEN TEST

CAST / CREW:

TITLE	DATE SEEN

CAST / CREW:

TITLE	DATE SEEN

CAST / CREW:

TITLE	DATE SEEN

T*here are lots of methods. Mine involves a lot of talent, a glass and some cracked ice.*

JOHN BARRYMORE

CAST / CREW:

TITLE	DATE SEEN

CAST / CREW:

TITLE	DATE SEEN

CAST / CREW:

TITLE	DATE SEEN

T he [Oscar] statuette is a perfect symbol of the picture business – a powerful athletic body clutching a gleaming sword, with half of his head, the part that holds his brains, completely sliced off. FRANCES MARION, 1928

CAST / CREW:

TITLE	DATE SEEN

GENRE:

TITLE	DATE SEEN

n certain pictures I do hope they will leave the cinema a little enriched, but I don't make them pay a buck and a half and then ram a lecture down their throats. BILLY WILDER

GENRE:

TITLE	DATE SEEN

GENRE:

TITLE	DATE SEEN

GENRE:

TITLE	DATE SEEN

GENRE:

TITLE	DATE SEEN

GENRE:	
TITLE	DATE SEEN

The Bible has been a bestseller for centuries. Why should I let two thousand years of publicity go to waste? CECIL B. DeMILLE

GENRE:

TITLE	DATE SEEN

GENRE:

TITLE   DATE SEEN

Take a chance and spend a million dollars and hope you're right. DARRYL F. ZANUCK

GENRE:

TITLE	DATE SEEN

GENRE:

TITLE	DATE SEEN

*T*he motion picture represents our customs and our daily life more distinctly than any other medium and, therefore, if we were to come back a thousand years from today and tried to find some form of expression that would more clearly, more perfectly explain how we live today, it would have to be the motion picture, because there is no medium of today that so universally must please as great a number of people... IRVING THALBERG, 1929

I'VE GOT THAT MOVIE HERE SOMEWHERE

MOVIE LIBRARY

TAPE NAME

VCR COUNTER NUMBER : START AT

MOVIE TITLE

TAPE NAME

VCR COUNTER NUMBER : START AT

MOVIE TITLE

TAPE NAME

VCR COUNTER NUMBER : START AT

MOVIE TITLE

TAPE NAME

VCR COUNTER NUMBER : START AT

MOVIE TITLE

TAPE NAME

VCR COUNTER NUMBER : START AT

MOVIE TITLE

TAPE NAME

VCR COUNTER NUMBER : START AT

MOVIE TITLE

TAPE NAME

VCR COUNTER NUMBER : START AT

MOVIE TITLE

MOVIE LIBRARY

TAPE NAME

VCR COUNTER NUMBER : START AT

MOVIE TITLE

TAPE NAME

VCR COUNTER NUMBER : START AT

MOVIE TITLE

TAPE NAME

VCR COUNTER NUMBER : START AT

MOVIE TITLE

TAPE NAME

VCR COUNTER NUMBER : START AT

MOVIE TITLE

TAPE NAME

VCR COUNTER NUMBER : START AT

MOVIE TITLE

TAPE NAME

VCR COUNTER NUMBER : START AT

MOVIE TITLE

TAPE NAME

VCR COUNTER NUMBER : START AT

MOVIE TITLE

TAPE NAME

VCR COUNTER NUMBER : START AT

MOVIE TITLE

TAPE NAME

VCR COUNTER NUMBER : START AT

MOVIE TITLE

TAPE NAME

VCR COUNTER NUMBER : START AT

MOVIE TITLE

TAPE NAME

VCR COUNTER NUMBER : START AT

MOVIE TITLE

TAPE NAME

VCR COUNTER NUMBER : START AT

MOVIE TITLE

*[*M*ovies are] an uncomfortable way of watching television.* SHEILA BLACK

MOVIE LIBRARY

TAPE NAME

VCR COUNTER NUMBER : START AT

MOVIE TITLE

TAPE NAME

VCR COUNTER NUMBER : START AT

MOVIE TITLE

TAPE NAME

VCR COUNTER NUMBER : START AT

MOVIE TITLE

TAPE NAME

VCR COUNTER NUMBER : START AT

MOVIE TITLE

TAPE NAME

VCR COUNTER NUMBER : START AT

MOVIE TITLE

TAPE NAME

VCR COUNTER NUMBER : START AT

MOVIE TITLE

TAPE NAME

VCR COUNTER NUMBER : START AT

MOVIE TITLE

MOVIE LIBRARY

TAPE NAME

VCR COUNTER NUMBER : START AT

MOVIE TITLE

TAPE NAME

VCR COUNTER NUMBER : START AT

MOVIE TITLE

TAPE NAME

VCR COUNTER NUMBER : START AT

MOVIE TITLE

TAPE NAME

VCR COUNTER NUMBER : START AT

MOVIE TITLE

TAPE NAME

VCR COUNTER NUMBER : START AT

MOVIE TITLE

TAPE NAME

VCR COUNTER NUMBER : START AT

MOVIE TITLE

TAPE NAME

VCR COUNTER NUMBER : START AT

MOVIE TITLE

MOVIE LIBRARY

TAPE NAME

VCR COUNTER NUMBER : START AT

MOVIE TITLE

TAPE NAME

VCR COUNTER NUMBER : START AT

MOVIE TITLE

TAPE NAME

VCR COUNTER NUMBER : START AT

MOVIE TITLE

TAPE NAME

VCR COUNTER NUMBER : START AT

MOVIE TITLE

TAPE NAME

VCR COUNTER NUMBER : START AT

MOVIE TITLE

TAPE NAME

VCR COUNTER NUMBER : START AT

MOVIE TITLE

TAPE NAME

VCR COUNTER NUMBER : START AT

MOVIE TITLE

TAPE NAME

VCR COUNTER NUMBER : START AT

MOVIE TITLE

TAPE NAME

VCR COUNTER NUMBER : START AT

MOVIE TITLE

TAPE NAME

VCR COUNTER NUMBER : START AT

MOVIE TITLE

TAPE NAME

VCR COUNTER NUMBER : START AT

MOVIE TITLE

TAPE NAME

VCR COUNTER NUMBER : START AT

MOVIE TITLE

TAPE NAME

VCR COUNTER NUMBER : START AT

MOVIE TITLE

TAPE NAME

VCR COUNTER NUMBER : START AT

MOVIE TITLE

TAPE NAME

VCR COUNTER NUMBER : START AT

MOVIE TITLE

TAPE NAME

VCR COUNTER NUMBER : START AT

MOVIE TITLE

TAPE NAME

VCR COUNTER NUMBER : START AT

MOVIE TITLE

TAPE NAME

VCR COUNTER NUMBER : START AT

MOVIE TITLE

TAPE NAME

VCR COUNTER NUMBER : START AT

MOVIE TITLE

*W*hy should people go out and pay money to see bad films when they can stay home and see bad television for nothing?*

SAMUEL GOLDWYN

MOVIE LIBRARY

TAPE NAME

VCR COUNTER NUMBER : START AT

MOVIE TITLE

TAPE NAME

VCR COUNTER NUMBER : START AT

MOVIE TITLE

TAPE NAME

VCR COUNTER NUMBER : START AT

MOVIE TITLE

TAPE NAME

VCR COUNTER NUMBER : START AT

MOVIE TITLE

TAPE NAME

VCR COUNTER NUMBER : START AT

MOVIE TITLE

TAPE NAME

VCR COUNTER NUMBER : START AT

MOVIE TITLE

TAPE NAME

VCR COUNTER NUMBER : START AT

MOVIE TITLE

MOVIE LIBRARY

TAPE NAME

VCR COUNTER NUMBER : START AT

MOVIE TITLE

TAPE NAME

VCR COUNTER NUMBER : START AT

MOVIE TITLE

TAPE NAME

VCR COUNTER NUMBER : START AT

MOVIE TITLE

TAPE NAME

VCR COUNTER NUMBER : START AT

MOVIE TITLE

TAPE NAME

VCR COUNTER NUMBER : START AT

MOVIE TITLE

TAPE NAME

VCR COUNTER NUMBER : START AT

MOVIE TITLE

TAPE NAME

VCR COUNTER NUMBER : START AT

MOVIE TITLE

Ninety-five percent of films are born of frustration, of self-despair, of ambition for survival, for money, for fattening bank accounts. Five percent, maybe less, are made because a man has an idea, an idea which he must express. SAMUEL FULLER

FILM
FESTIVALS

DATE:

FILM   THEATER / TIME

DATE:

FILM	THEATER / TIME

make movies to show that this is not the best of all possible worlds. LUIS BUNUEL

TITLE

CAST / CREW

STUDIO / YEAR

THEATER / DATE / TIME

REVIEW

TITLE

CAST / CREW

STUDIO / YEAR

THEATER / DATE / TIME

REVIEW

O f course, a film should have a beginning, a middle and an end. But not necessarily in that order. JEAN-LUC GODARD

TITLE

CAST / CREW

STUDIO / YEAR

THEATER / DATE / TIME

REVIEW

TITLE

CAST / CREW

STUDIO / YEAR

THEATER / DATE / TIME

REVIEW

TITLE

CAST / CREW

STUDIO / YEAR

THEATER / DATE / TIME

REVIEW

TITLE

CAST / CREW

STUDIO / YEAR

THEATER / DATE / TIME

REVIEW

TITLE

CAST / CREW

STUDIO / YEAR

THEATER / DATE / TIME

REVIEW

TITLE

CAST / CREW

STUDIO / YEAR

THEATER / DATE / TIME

REVIEW

TITLE

CAST / CREW

STUDIO / YEAR

THEATER / DATE / TIME

REVIEW

TITLE

CAST / CREW

STUDIO / YEAR

THEATER / DATE / TIME

REVIEW

ell, goodbye, Mr. Zanuck. And let me tell you, it certainly has been a pleasure working at Sixteenth Century Fox.

JEAN RENOIR

TITLE

CAST / CREW

STUDIO / YEAR

THEATER / DATE / TIME

REVIEW

TITLE

CAST / CREW

STUDIO / YEAR

THEATER / DATE / TIME

REVIEW

TITLE

CAST / CREW

STUDIO / YEAR

THEATER / DATE / TIME

REVIEW

TITLE

CAST / CREW

STUDIO / YEAR

THEATER / DATE / TIME

REVIEW

TITLE

CAST / CREW

STUDIO / YEAR

THEATER / DATE / TIME

REVIEW

film is a tapeworm, a tapeworm 2,500 metres long that sucks the life and spirit out of me. INGMAR BERGMAN

TITLE

CAST / CREW

STUDIO / YEAR

THEATER / DATE / TIME

REVIEW

TITLE

CAST / CREW

STUDIO / YEAR

THEATER / DATE / TIME

REVIEW

TITLE

CAST / CREW

STUDIO / YEAR

THEATER / DATE / TIME

REVIEW

TITLE

CAST / CREW

STUDIO / YEAR

THEATER / DATE / TIME

REVIEW

TITLE

CAST / CREW

STUDIO / YEAR

THEATER / DATE / TIME

REVIEW

Keep it out of focus. I want to win the foreign-picture award. BILLY WILDER

don't care for modern films – all crash-ing cars and close-ups of people's feet.

LILLIAN GISH

There never was a silent film. We'd finish a picture, show it in one of our projection rooms and come out shattered. It would be awful. Then we'd show it in a theater with a girl pounding away at a piano and there would be all the difference in the world. Without that music there wouldn't have been a movie industry at all. IRVING THALBERG

THE
SUPPORTING
CAST

TITLE

AUTHOR

SUBJECT

PUBLISHER / PUB. DATE

NOTES

TITLE

AUTHOR

SUBJECT

PUBLISHER / PUB. DATE

NOTES

TITLE

AUTHOR

SUBJECT

PUBLISHER / PUB. DATE

NOTES

TITLE

AUTHOR

SUBJECT

PUBLISHER / PUB. DATE

NOTES

TITLE

AUTHOR

SUBJECT

PUBLISHER / PUB. DATE

NOTES

TITLE

AUTHOR

SUBJECT

PUBLISHER / PUB. DATE

NOTES

TITLE

AUTHOR

SUBJECT

PUBLISHER / PUB. DATE

NOTES

TITLE

AUTHOR

SUBJECT

PUBLISHER / PUB. DATE

NOTES

TITLE

AUTHOR

SUBJECT

PUBLISHER / PUB. DATE

NOTES

TITLE

AUTHOR

SUBJECT

PUBLISHER / PUB. DATE

NOTES

TITLE

AUTHOR

SUBJECT

PUBLISHER / PUB. DATE

NOTES

TITLE

AUTHOR

SUBJECT

PUBLISHER / PUB. DATE

NOTES

TITLE

AUTHOR

SUBJECT

PUBLISHER / PUB. DATE

NOTES

TITLE

AUTHOR

SUBJECT

PUBLISHER / PUB. DATE

NOTES

TITLE

AUTHOR

SUBJECT

PUBLISHER / PUB. DATE

NOTES

f my books had been any worse, I should not have been invited to Hollywood, and if they had been any better, I should not have come.

RAYMOND CHANDLER

AUTHOR	TITLE

AUTHOR	TITLE

As long past as 1930, I had a hunch that the talkies would make even the bestselling novelist as archaic as silent pictures. F. SCOTT FITZGERALD

SUBJECT:

TITLE	AUTHOR

he films take our best ideas. We work like slaves, inventing, devising, changing, to please the morons who run this game. We spend endless hours in search of novel ideas, and, in the end, what do we get? A lousy fortune! CHRISTOPHER ISHERWOOD

MOVIE BOOKS BY SUBJECT

SUBJECT:

TITLE	AUTHOR

TITLE

ADDRESS / PHONE

SUBSCRIPTION #

SUBSCRIPTION BEGINS / ENDS

TITLE

ADDRESS / PHONE

SUBSCRIPTION #

SUBSCRIPTION BEGINS / ENDS

TITLE

ADDRESS / PHONE

SUBSCRIPTION #

SUBSCRIPTION BEGINS / ENDS

TITLE

ADDRESS / PHONE

SUBSCRIPTION #

SUBSCRIPTION BEGINS / ENDS

TITLE

ADDRESS / PHONE

SUBSCRIPTION #

SUBSCRIPTION BEGINS / ENDS

MOVIE MAGAZINES

TITLE

ADDRESS / PHONE

SUBSCRIPTION #

SUBSCRIPTION BEGINS / ENDS

TITLE

ADDRESS / PHONE

SUBSCRIPTION #

SUBSCRIPTION BEGINS / ENDS

TITLE

ADDRESS / PHONE

SUBSCRIPTION #

SUBSCRIPTION BEGINS / ENDS

TITLE

ADDRESS / PHONE

SUBSCRIPTION #

SUBSCRIPTION BEGINS / ENDS

TITLE

ADDRESS / PHONE

SUBSCRIPTION #

SUBSCRIPTION BEGINS / ENDS

MOVIE TITLE

MUSIC

ARTISTS

LABEL / YEAR

REVIEW / NOTES

MOVIE TITLE

MUSIC

ARTISTS

LABEL / YEAR

REVIEW / NOTES

MOVIE TITLE

MUSIC

ARTISTS

LABEL / YEAR

REVIEW / NOTES

MOVIE TITLE

MUSIC

ARTISTS

LABEL / YEAR

REVIEW / NOTES

MOVIE MUSIC

MOVIE TITLE

MUSIC

ARTISTS

LABEL / YEAR

REVIEW / NOTES

MOVIE TITLE

MUSIC

ARTISTS

LABEL / YEAR

REVIEW / NOTES

MOVIE TITLE

MUSIC

ARTISTS

LABEL / YEAR

REVIEW / NOTES

t will never be possible to synchronize the voice with the pictures. Music— fine music— will always be the voice of silent drama... There will never be silent films. D.W. GRIFFITH, 1924

MOVIE TITLE

MUSIC

ARTISTS

LABEL / YEAR

REVIEW / NOTES

MOVIE TITLE

MUSIC

ARTISTS

LABEL / YEAR

REVIEW / NOTES

MOVIE TITLE

MUSIC

ARTISTS

LABEL / YEAR

REVIEW / NOTES

MOVIE TITLE

MUSIC

ARTISTS

LABEL / YEAR

REVIEW / NOTES

MOVIE MUSIC

MOVIE TITLE

MUSIC

ARTISTS

LABEL / YEAR

REVIEW / NOTES

MOVIE TITLE

MUSIC

ARTISTS

LABEL / YEAR

REVIEW / NOTES

MOVIE TITLE

MUSIC

ARTISTS

LABEL / YEAR

REVIEW / NOTES

MOVIE TITLE

MUSIC

ARTISTS

LABEL / YEAR

REVIEW / NOTES

You can take all the sincerity of Hollywood, place it in the navel of a fruit fly and still have room enough for three caraway seeds and a producer's heart.

FRED ALLEN

YOU'VE GOT TO SEE THIS MOVIE

MOVIES BORROWED

TITLE

CAST / CREW

LENDER

DATE BORROWED   DATE RETURNED

TITLE

CAST / CREW

LENDER

DATE BORROWED   DATE RETURNED

TITLE

CAST / CREW

LENDER

DATE BORROWED   DATE RETURNED

TITLE

CAST / CREW

LENDER

DATE BORROWED   DATE RETURNED

TITLE

CAST / CREW

LENDER

DATE BORROWED   DATE RETURNED

MOVIES BORROWED

TITLE

CAST / CREW

LENDER

DATE BORROWED   DATE RETURNED

TITLE

CAST / CREW

LENDER

DATE BORROWED   DATE RETURNED

TITLE

CAST / CREW

LENDER

DATE BORROWED   DATE RETURNED

TITLE

CAST / CREW

LENDER

DATE BORROWED   DATE RETURNED

TITLE

CAST / CREW

LENDER

DATE BORROWED   DATE RETURNED

TITLE

CAST / CREW

BORROWER

DATE LOANED   DATE RETURNED

TITLE

CAST / CREW

BORROWER

DATE LOANED   DATE RETURNED

TITLE

CAST / CREW

BORROWER

DATE LOANED   DATE RETURNED

TITLE

CAST / CREW

BORROWER

DATE LOANED   DATE RETURNED

[**H** ollywood is] *a place where they shoot too many pictures and not enough actors.* WALTER WINCHELL

MOVIES LOANED

TITLE

CAST / CREW

BORROWER

DATE LOANED   DATE RETURNED

TITLE

CAST / CREW

BORROWER

DATE LOANED   DATE RETURNED

TITLE

CAST / CREW

BORROWER

DATE LOANED   DATE RETURNED

TITLE

CAST / CREW

BORROWER

DATE LOANED   DATE RETURNED

TITLE ·

CAST / CREW

BORROWER

DATE LOANED   DATE RETURNED

MOVIES TO GIVE AS GIFTS

MOVIE LOVER	GIFT IDEAS

MOVIE LOVER	GIFT IDEAS

MOVIE LOVER

OCCASION

MOVIE TITLE

MOVIE LOVER

OCCASION

MOVIE TITLE

MOVIE LOVER

OCCASION

MOVIE TITLE

MOVIE LOVER

OCCASION

MOVIE TITLE

T o survive in Hollywood you need: the ambition of a Latin-American revolutionary; the ego of a grand opera tenor; and the physical stamina of a cow pony. BILLIE BURKE

MOVIES GIVEN AS GIFTS

MOVIE LOVER

OCCASION

MOVIE TITLE

MOVIE LOVER

OCCASION

MOVIE TITLE

MOVIE LOVER

OCCASION

MOVIE TITLE

MOVIE LOVER

OCCASION

MOVIE TITLE

MOVIE LOVER

OCCASION

MOVIE TITLE

MOVIE LOVER

OCCASION

MOVIE TITLE

MOVIE LOVER

OCCASION

MOVIE TITLE

MOVIES RECEIVED AS GIFTS

MOVIE TITLE

FROM

OCCASION

MOVIE TITLE

FROM

OCCASION

MOVIE TITLE

FROM

OCCASION

MOVIE TITLE

FROM

OCCASION

MOVIE TITLE

FROM

OCCASION

MOVIE TITLE

FROM

OCCASION

MOVIE TITLE

FROM

OCCASION

MOVIES RECEIVED AS GIFTS

MOVIE TITLE

FROM

OCCASION

MOVIE TITLE

FROM

OCCASION

MOVIE TITLE

FROM

OCCASION

MOVIE TITLE

FROM

OCCASION

MOVIE TITLE

FROM

OCCASION

t's such nonsense, this immorality of Hollywood. We're all too tired. ROBERT LORD

T he cynics are always with us — those who say Hollywood cannot face reality, that everything must be glossed over and made unreal. What the cynics do not realize is that dreams are often more real than reality. There is a reality beyond that which we see and touch and feel. There exists within man a groping toward an idealistic extension of himself, an undefeatable belief that life can be pleasanter than it may be at the moment, a staunch conviction that there are possibilities beyond his own narrow horizons. The movie with the fairytale, Cinderella, happy-ending plot brings joy because it also brings hope. MERVYN LEROY

MOVIE
LISTS

MOST-WATCHED MOVIES

have gone to the movies constantly, and at times, almost compulsively for most of my life. I should be embarrassed to attempt an estimate of how many movies I have seen and how many hours they have consumed.

ROBERT WARSHOW

TOP-TEN MOVIE LIST

TOP-TEN MOVIE LIST

CHILDHOOD FAVORITES

t was an aroma compounded of plush and worn carpet and Devon violets and sweat. It was that scent, perhaps, which first made me a film fan; for it was to the Queen's in Bolton that I ventured on my first remembered visit to any cinema, one wet and windy afternoon in 1933, when I was four. LESLIE HALLIWELL

T hey say the movies should be more
like life – I think life should be more
like the movies. MYRNA LOY

FAVORITE PERFORMANCES

would like to think what I'm capturing is some reflection of the truth of what our lives are like, and yet, on that desert island, I don't want to see that truth. I want to see the dream of what life could be like. I want to see Ginger Rogers' dresses and Fred Astaire's feet move – see him dance the night away and keep falling in love with that same perfect woman – and never have it go wrong because we never get to the sixth reel. HENRY JAGLOM

DESERT ISLAND MOVIES

T

ravesties of religious rites...references to royalty...hangings or executions either serious or comic... political propaganda...too much shooting...intoxication...cruelty... companionate marriage...free love...immodesty...vamping... vulgar noises...harsh screams...the divinity...life after death...British officers shown in an unflattering light... THEMES BANNED BY THE BRITISH CENSOR, 1930

FAVORITE
MOVIE
LINES

FAVORITE MOVIE LINES

t is in the interest of the producers to maintain a certain moral standard since, if they don't do this, the immoral films won't sell. JEAN RENOIR

FAVORITE MOVIE LINES

Make no mistake, the almost chemical effect with which a good motion picture alters the mood of its audience can be dissipated or destroyed if it is shown in the wrong physical setting...The fun of movie-going includes more than just seeing the film. It is the subtle blending of a series of pleasurable stimuli – the initial anticipation, the feeling of elegance, the congeniality of the surroundings – these are what establish the final satisfaction, the total experience.

GARTH DRABINSKY

MOVIE
PALACES

MOVIE THEATERS

NAME

ADDRESS

PHONE

NOTES

NAME

ADDRESS

PHONE

NOTES

NAME

ADDRESS

PHONE

NOTES

NAME

ADDRESS

PHONE

NOTES

NAME

ADDRESS

PHONE

NOTES

MOVIE THEATERS

NAME

ADDRESS

PHONE

NOTES

NAME

ADDRESS

PHONE

NOTES

NAME

ADDRESS

PHONE

NOTES

NAME

ADDRESS

PHONE

NOTES

NAME

ADDRESS

PHONE

NOTES

VIDEO STORES

NAME

ADDRESS

PHONE

NOTES

NAME

ADDRESS

PHONE

NOTES

NAME

ADDRESS

PHONE

NOTES

NAME

ADDRESS

PHONE

NOTES

NAME

ADDRESS

PHONE

NOTES

VIDEO STORES

NAME

ADDRESS

PHONE

NOTES

NAME

ADDRESS

PHONE

NOTES

NAME

ADDRESS

PHONE

NOTES

NAME

ADDRESS

PHONE

NOTES

The length of the film should be directly related to the endurance of the human bladder. ALFRED HITCHCOCK

NAME

VENUE / DATES

PHONE

NOTES

NAME

VENUE / DATES

PHONE

NOTES

NAME

VENUE / DATES

PHONE

NOTES

NAME

VENUE / DATES

PHONE

NOTES

f you want art, don't mess around with movies – buy a Picasso. MICHAEL WINNER